Understanding & Implementing Development

by Richard J. Burke

**National Catholic
Educational
Association
Office of Development**

Table of Contents

About the Author

Richard J. Burke is a native of New Haven who currently resides in Madison, Connecticut. He attended New Haven public elementary schools and Notre Dame High School in West Haven, Connecticut. He holds a Bachelor of Science degree in Business Economics and Finance from the University of Bridgeport and has done graduate work in economics and marketing at UB. Richard is married to Arlene (Shaw) formerly of New Haven. They have four children.

Prior to his full-time involvement with Catholic schools, Mr. Burke served the Olin Corporation in financial and market planning departments for four years. Beginning with Olin as a Financial Analyst in 1969, he left Olin in 1973 as Manager of Marketing Research.

The National Catholic Educational Association formally endorsed Richard J. Burke as the NCEA Financial Planning Consultant for Catholic schools and parishes in January, 1978. Since December, 1975 he has served as Business Planning Coordinator for the Archdiocese of Hartford, Connecticut. Through Richard J. Burke & Associates, he has provided consultative services to parochial, private and diocesan elementary and secondary schools and parishes since 1969.

During 1973-74 he served as a consultant to the Archbishop's study committee on parish councils, assisting in drafting revised guidelines for parish councils in the Archdiocese of Hartford in late 1974. Mr. Burke has conducted hundreds of workshops and seminars in more than seventy dioceses throughout the country and has served as a lecturer and instructor for the Institute for Catholic Educational Leadership at the University of San Francisco.

Since 1979, Mr. Burke has written and published the *Catholic School Management Letter*. The *Catholic School Management Letter,* published four times annually, is designed as a tool for pastors, principals and School Board members, dealing with finance and management issues for Catholic schools.

Mr. Burke has served on the Advisory Council for the Sisters of Notre Dame de Namur; the Board of Directors for Notre Dame High School, West Haven; St. George Parish Council Finance Committee; and the National Catholic Educational Association Finance and Planning Committees. He is also a member of the Hartford Association of Business Economists.

Foreword

The material presented in "Understanding & Implementing Development" was presented as the keynote of the first development symposium sponsored by the National Catholic Educational Association in Boston, MA, April 23-26, 1984. This booklet describes the earliest phases of planning a development program. It poses many of the questions that must be faced as one approaches development.

Mr. Burke's original presentation was verbal. In an attempt to prepare this material for printed format, it has not been possible to eliminate all personal references. Rather than destroy the personal sense of the message, the editor has determined to keep the original personal style. The reader is asked to proceed with this in mind. Much of the discussion following the presentation added a great deal to further understanding. It is not possible to capture all the enthusiasm of that exchange on these pages.

The forms suggested for planning in Appendix B are much too small to be workable. The same forms are available in 8-1/2″ × 11″ format as an Appendix to a larger book entitled *Elementary School Finance Manual*. Those interested may obtain this book from the Publications Sales Office, NCEA. The cost is $10.00.

Mr. Burke has generously and competently worked for the benefit of Catholic institutions since 1978. Through planning techniques which he promotes, many institutions are now serving their constituents in a more responsible manner. I am grateful to Mr. Burke for the dedication and professionalism he brings to his work.

Reverend Robert J. Yeager
Vice President/Development
December 1, 1984

Understanding & Implementing Development

Richard J. Burke

One pastor recently met with his elementary school principal and said, "I've been reading about the need for development in private schools. Development programs can bring in a good deal of money and so I would like you to hire a development director. Please tell the development director to find out what development is and do it. We need money."

Unfortunately, such an approach usually will not produce the desired results. Development efforts, to be successful, depend on broad-based understanding and commitment, as well as an expanded level of involvement and long-range planning.

This booklet is designed to place development within a proper perspective.

Development, as used throughout this booklet, is defined by Gonser Gerber Tinker Stuhr of Chicago as follows:

*"The overall concept of development
holds that the highest destiny of an institution
can be realized only by a total effort
on the part of the institution
to analyze its educational or programmatic philosophy
and activities,
to crystallize its objectives,
project them into the future,
and take the necessary steps to realize them."*[1]

---

[1]Gonser Gerber Tinker Stuhr, *On Development* (Chicago: Gonser Gerber Tinker Stuhr, 1977), p.4.

Today there is growing interest in planning and development for dioceses as well as for Catholic elementary and secondary schools. This interest is due largely to the scenario that was prevalent during the period 1964 to 1972 in almost 20% of the Catholic schools nationally: schools were going to be closed at the end of the current school year primarily as a result of increasing financial pressures, a decline in the numbers of Religious available to staff and administer those schools, and increasing pressure on parent and student fund raising to produce dollars lost by decreases in parish subsidy. Although the number of Catholic school closings has declined, the factors cited above call for increased emphasis on development activities.

In the latter half of the 1980's and certainly in the 1990's there is a multi-tiered financing mix that includes not only some combination of traditional tuitions plus parish subsidies plus fund raising, but at a fourth leg of that mix: development   sophisticated, researched, planned, formal development efforts.[2] Our approach to development cannot be one that says we simply need to raise more dollars by concentrating on grantsmanship, corporate gifts, remainder trusts, lead trusts, and the like, rather than on candy sales, car raffles and bingos. It cannot simply be an attempt to raise dollars in a somewhat more sophisticated way, if in fact that's the right term. There needs to be an initial understanding of and commitment to where we're going. This booklet will outline what are believed to be the most successful steps in insuring that development programs can in fact work for your school.

Understanding   In order for development programs to work, that is, to attract friends, and to bring in dollars over the long term, there initially needs to be a common, basic understanding on the part of all of those people involved in the leadership of the school. In a parish school that leadership would involve the pastor, the principal and the board. In a diocesan-owned or regional school, that leadership would include the super-

---

[2]"Financing Strategies for the 1980's," *Catholic School Management Letter,* Volume I, No. 1, May 1979. Catholic School Management, 24 Cornfield Lane, Madison, CT 06443.

intendent as well as the diocesan fiscal officer, the principal and the school board. Those individuals, at the very least, need to have an understanding of two things that are of paramount importance in making the development program work: (1) an understanding of the basic concept of development; and (2) an understanding of the philosophy of a Catholic school and its unique mission.

Definition of Development

Development is not synonymous with fund raising: it does not attempt to initially attract dollars to insure the survival of the school.[3] Rather development attracts friends to insure that the school is living up to its mission. This concept of development was originally penned by the development consulting firm of Gonser Gerber Tinker Stuhr of Chicago. This concept holds that the highest destiny of a school can be realized only by a total effort on its part to analyze its philosophy and mission, to crystallize its objectives, project them into the future and to take the necessary steps to insure that those objectives are realized. This definition also underlies the development program recommended by the National Catholic Educational Association for parishes, schools and dioceses throughout the country.

Institutional Philosophy

Development is not simply a process; it is a concept. Development assumes a long-term effort and the involvement of people. It starts with an analysis and review of the philosophy and mission statement of the school. As we look at the understanding on the part of the principal, the board, and the pastor, we consider the second major component of understanding that is prerequisite to effective development: an understanding of the philosophy of Catholic school and its unique mission. As I work with schools in their planning and development efforts, I frequently spend time with faculty members talking to them about why it is important that they not simply be the best science teacher or the best history teacher, the best kindergarten or third grade teacher, but why

---

[3]"Development Versus Fund Raising," *Catholic School Management Letter,* Volume II, No. 2, September, 1980. Catholic School Management, 24 Cornfield Lane, Madison, CT 06443.

they need to become part of the development process itself. It is important that teachers, as well as parents, understand how the school can remain Catholic, survive and flourish even when there are no longer Sisters available to staff and administer that school. That understanding comes out of the philosophy of a Catholic education that suggests that the primary component of that education is an integration of faith with the learning process, and that all of the other components—the religion program, the campus ministry program, the basic curriculum areas and extracurricular activities are supportive. In short, it is necessary initially that there be an understanding of both the philosophy of a Catholic school education and the development concept in order to make development work.

School Mission

Beyond philosophy there also needs to be a clear understanding of the school's particular mission. Many individual schools will have philosophies that are basically identical. The philosophy will talk about an integration of faith with life and learning, about the education of the whole child, education for justice, and education for global awareness. Mission statements however, will be dramatically different in many cases. The mission statement identifies the school as unique; it talks about who you are and why you're there. It responds to the question: "If the school burned down tonight, would it reopen in September, and why?" To put it another way, the philosophy talks about what the school is called to *be*. The mission statement talks about what the school is called to *do*, who it is to serve, and who in fact it cannot serve. Finally, the mission statement sets the tone for your development program: it gives you an opportunity to talk to people about why the school is important, not simply to the two hundred students that are there—or two thousand—but to the numerous publics that the school ought to be reporting to on a regular and consistent basis.

Beyond even philosophy and mission statement, specific objectives need to be stated for each class or department, as well as the overall objectives for the school. These objectives should be stated in terms of who we're attempting to serve, who we simply cannot serve, and how schools begin to be expanded through development efforts. Summarily, it is critical that in beginning any development program, the pastor, the principal, and the board sit down and look specifically at the concept of development and the philosophy and mission statement of the school. But that is not enough.

Commitment Step number two in a successful development program is to internalize that understanding, to make it real, and to make it a part of what you are doing on a day-to-day basis, whether you are pastor, principal, board member, superintendent or teacher. In other words, individuals, must make a concerted effort to create a level of commitment that says we are going to stay with this. This process is long-term and ongoing.

Anyone going into a development program needs to realize initially that in order to receive substantial benefits from the attraction of both people and dollars, the process, on average, takes at least three years. You are posturing the school for a long-term survival and hopefully an ability to not simply survive but to flourish. The commitment should be broad-based. Development cannot be a commitment simply on the part of the principal nor the chairperson of the school board. There needs to be an understanding of and a commitment to both the concept of development and the philosophy of the school, on the part of the pastor, principal and board. That usually only takes place through an education process, sometimes referred to as a preservice.

Preserve of Personnel

It is important that we look at that preservice as one of the primary prerequisites for development. Take time to share with the board members, the pastor, the principal. and with faculty members, what development is, why it is not synonymous with fund raising, and why they too need to talk about the reasons for the school's success. The question is frequently asked in individual sessions with schools, "What do you do if the school is already full—we don't need to recruit students, we don't need a capital campaign, the school has a balanced budget." Never cease to market that school for image, even if the classes are at capacity and there are families on the waiting list. The fact is that you need to make a commitment that is long term. You do not need simply to solve the problems that exist today, but to seek out, to find, and in many cases to create the opportunities that should be there for your school in the years ahead. It is the opportunity not simply to market for enrollment or dollars, but to tell people why your school is important and why, even in a community where the public schools are exceptionally good, Catholic schools are not only important, they're critical. In short, we want also to market the image of the school. It is up to us—parents, principals, Board members and pastors—to insure that Catholic schools not simply survive but flourish. Both understanding and commitment precede my formal development efforts on the public side.

Commitment comes from understanding and understanding comes from education and awareness.

Involvement   The third prerequisite in this process is a level of involvement. This involvement is the single, most critical component of successful development programs, whether they be at the diocesan, the parish, the elementary or secondary school level. There is a long list of those who should be involved. I have occasionally heard pastors ask, "If I as pastor want the development program and my principal does not want to be involved, will it work?" I have also heard the other side: "As principal, I think we need a development program; however, the pastor does not want any part of it." And I've heard a similar cry from boards: "I cannot get active involvement on the part of. . ." I submit at the outset that the involvement of *all* of those individuals is in fact important to successful development programs. While a program can work to varying degrees when the emphasis and the involvement is stronger with only one of the parties, like a play, it is most successful when the entire cast of characters works together. There should be involvement initially by the principal, by the pastor, by the school board and, in fact, by the faculty members. Teachers should not be excluded but should be involved and told that in order for development programs to be successful they should be remarkable educators, as well as representatives of and spokespersons for their school. It is the successful teacher who can more than anyone else create investment opportunities. It is the teacher who more than anyone else can relate to parents. It is the teacher who can bring to the board a perspective that no one else can. A story illustrates this point.

In addition to my consulting and administrative responsibilities I make it a point to sit on at least one elementary and one secondary school board on an ongoing basis. This allows me to see from several different perspectives the workings of Catholic schools. When I was first appointed to an elementary school board I arrived at the first meeting with a folder of information on five-year plans, on development programs, on the school's need for an endowment. I was also prepared that evening to introduce a calendarized budget and cash flow system. The agenda had not been sent out in advance and I was more than a little bit disturbed to arrive to find out that the first hour of the meeting was devoted to an inservice for the board presented by the kindergarten teacher.

The kindergarten teacher was supposedly going to tell us what it was like to be a teacher in kindergarten in the school and to suggest, as it said on the agenda, some policy considerations. I couldn't believe I was giving up another night to listen to this and not to discuss the extremely important financial and development information I had. At any rate, I sat there and, in fact, it may have been one of the most informative and enlightening evenings I've ever spent. Even as I talk to people about the need to understand the philosophy and mission of the school, I had not internalized it until I sat and listened to that kindergarten teacher talk about policy needs. She said in part, "We need policies in this school that deal not only with financial priorities and the collection of tuition—you may get to those—but rather we need a policy that says that birthday party invitations may not be given out in school, going to school or coming from school. And if as parents you want to have a party for your child and you want to invite classmates, give me, the teacher, the invitations. We talk in the school's philosophy about education for justice, the education of the whole child, about building faith into all that we do. Do you have any idea what it's like to stand there in a class of fifteen and watch while seven party invitations are given out." The impact that particular statement made on the board was probably one of the most significant, even from a development perspective, that has ever been made.

It is not simply *what* we do every day in the school, whether we be pastor, principal, board member or kindergarten teacher; it's also *how* we project that to the various publics that we purport to serve: students, families, and the other people with whom we come in contact. In short, it is imperative that faculty members be involved at the very outset of a development program, and that they understand the concept of development structured within the philosophy of the school. There is a key role for faculty members to play not simply in the writing of investment opportunities later on, but in terms of policy determination and inservice at the outset. Finally, in addition to faculty, we seek to involve, parents, alumni, grandparents, local businesses and others. However, before we get to the expansion of involvement there needs to be some semblance of order, a sense that we know where we're going and how we're going to get there. Step number four in this process involves planning.

Planning

It is important for administrators and board to develop formal, written, long-range plans—usually defined as five year plans—that do not simply state financial projections, but involve the entire operation of the school. This planning process attempts to look five years ahead in terms of the school's philosophy, mission, enrollment, staffing, curriculum, plant and facilities, finances, and its directional goals with regard to development. Without a formal long-range plan you run the risk later on, as you begin to cultivate ever increasing numbers of publics, of having those individuals come into the school and raise questions like: "Why are we doing what we're doing?" "Why can't we find an alternative source of income besides this particular foundation for our funding needs?" "Why is the program structured as it is?" "Why is this school perceived as comprehensive and not college preparatory?" "Why, in an elementary school that has this philosophy, is there no provision made in the curriculum for music, or physical education, or art?" If we attempt to answer those questions only from a financial perspective (i.e. we do not have special programs because we cannot afford it), we do a genuine disservice to the future of the school. Within the planning process, we turn that around to say that we need this program and in fact we can afford it with help and with resources — human and financial, internal and external. Good Development Planning invites participation.

The long-range plan is designed not to be simply an end in itself. It is designed to be the foundation on which you build a successful development program. This year I finished some initial consulting with a Catholic college, a small four-year liberal arts school. As the school began to look at long-range planning for the first time, it realized that it was not able to say where it was going or why it wanted to go in a particular direction. What the school needed was not so much a long-range plan that looked at enrollment and staffing, curriculum, plant and facilities and finances. Rather, it needed a strategic plan that addressed fundamental issues about who they were and why they existed. Without that clarity they were going to have severe problems in projecting in any of the other areas—enrollment, staffing and so forth.

For most Catholic elementary and secondary schools a strategic plan is not necessary, but a five-year plan is critical. Without this plan development efforts will be severely hampered. You will certainly hinder your ability to attract increasing numbers of donors, as well as your efforts to seek foundation and corporate support. The five-year plan for any school is designed largely to be an internal document, a road map, a guide for the pastor, the principal, the board, and the superintendent. It tells the leadership where the school is going and how it is going to get there. The five-year plan provides the basis for an external document, the Case Statement. The fifth step in the process is the development of that Case Statement. (cf. Long-Range Plan Guidelines—Appendix B)

The Case Statement

A Case Statement, simply defined, is a document for public consumption, drawn out of the five-year plan.[4] It is based on and reflective of that plan. The Case Statement talks to people outside of the school community about who you are, why you're there and why this particular ministry is so important. It expresses the need and desire for public involvement not only in terms of dollars, but in terms of human resources as well. The Case also expresses why the goals you seek to achieve cannot be achieved unless there is that involvement. A Case Statement is more than a brochure that is put together on glossy paper with pictures in full color. A Case Statement

---

[4]"Preparing an Effective Case Statement," *Catholic School Management Letter,* Vol. V, No. 2, September, 1983. Catholic School Management, 24 Cornfield Lane, Madison, CT 06443.

fundamentally and most importantly is a rough draft on 8-1/2 × 11 paper that goes through a whole series of drafts. It is that particular part of the Case Statement—the rewriting and reviewing that makes the Case worthwhile.

A Case Statement is usually prepared by someone in the school—a teacher, an administrator, a board member. It is based on and reflective of the long-range plan. It is written not from an internal perspective; that is, not in terms of, "We are St. Bernadette's and we would like to tell you about us." It is written from an external perspective; that is, "This is how we would like you to become involved in St. Bernadette's." "You" can be parent, grandparent, alum, foundation, corporation or friend. The Case is a targeted document; that is, it specifies that it is being written largely for grandparents or for corporate donors. And it is written from *their* perspective.

The Case needs to be presented both in terms of opportunities and in terms of restrictions on resources. It is important that the draft of the Case go through several revisions. It is also important that there be no pride of authorship. It is a team effort: "I have written this Case and I would now like to give it to the Board members for their critique and input.". . . "This is how we see the school and these are the elements that we think should be emphasized. This is the story that we should tell." The Case Statement, more than anything else provides the information necessary for attracting both human and financial resources to the school.

This leads us to step number six in the funding piece—the attraction of dollars over a period of time to the school, whether those dollars be annual dollars, capital dollars or endowed dollars.

Funding

In looking at an overview of this kind of development, it is important that we differentiate the kinds of dollars that we are eventually going to attract. When I initially met the representatives of Gonser Gerber Tinker Stuhr, under whose development definition we're working, I was impressed with Robert Tinker who was then one of the senior consultants of the firm and now retired. He talked to me at length about the need to forget about dollars at the outset; about the need to look to people whether they be parents, board members, or friends. We spent time finding out who they were and why they were interested in that particular school. He went on to say that, "The fact of the matter is, whether it's a college, a high school, an elementary school, a Montessori school, or a day-care program—people respond to people and not to institutions; people give to people more than they give to institutions. If you're committed to development, find opportunities to meet people outside of the school setting, find out where they are in relation to that school, and what they feel are the most important elements in the school's survival. It's only with that kind of people involvement that you can eventually generate funding through several different sources."

When I talk to faculty members initially about development in their schools I ask them to sit together for awhile and develop a "wish list": "Tell me what you would like to see in the school if money were no obstacle? what would it take to make sure that you had everything that you wanted in order to educate in the most effective ways?" From that "wish list" investment opportunities are created.[5] Not all of us think or feel the same way. Some of us will respond very well to opportunities in terms of foreign languages in the elementary school. Others have no interest at all in that program, but are vitally interested in creating an expanded physical education program. Others are interested in upgrading science programs. If the faculty members cannot get excited about the programs in the school they are not going to be in a position to sell them outside.

Annual giving programs should initially be considered in order to build support for the school, to attract new donors, to make sure that these people have an opportunity year after year to become involved in the school. Annual Giving responds not simply to the problems that exist, but rather to the opportunities that are presented. The annual giving program should be structured in such a way that it does not simply bring in dollars, but attracts people. Efforts should be made to get to know the individuals who invest in the school, whether the investment be dollars or time. Look at why certain individuals are committed to and willing to invest in that particular school and why other individuals are not. That takes time and effort, as well as careful organization. It takes an ability to

---

[5]"Creating and Funding Investment Opportunities," *Catholic School Management Letter,* Volume IV, No. 3, December, 1982. Catholic School Management 24 Cornfield Lane, Madison, CT 06443.

put together information in a usable format. In short, there is a need to be somewhat systematized in your development efforts.

Use of Volunteers

Many have volunteers working in these institutions. How often we find individuals, particularly senior citizens, who come into the school and say, "I would like to help." We very often don't have places for them. Or conversely, we have not gone out and provided the opportunity for individuals to be involved in the school. I encourage you to create those opportunities. In one elementary school office there are three senior citizens who come in. They are invited to come in for one or two mornings a week and have coffee and read the newspaper. These women provide an invaluable service. They go through the newspapers—locals, dailies, nationals—and they clip articles on *people*. Most of us read the society or regional pages, the obituaries or the business news. Soon the information is forgotten. If you buy into a process that says you will crystallize objectives and follow through, there needs to be organization. Clip those articles, file them and cross-reference them. In that way, when you have an opportunity to talk to an individual about a particular program, you will know if he has received a promotion or if his daughter has recently been married. People respond to people more than to institutions. Development efforts need to be structured in such a way as to exhibit a sense of caring. I am very frequently told by administrators, "I don't have time to do what you're suggesting." None of us do. That is not a problem—that is an opportunity. The ladies who come in and provide the clipping service described above are learning about the schools—about Catholic education. They're seeing first-hand what is happening. They are involved. Recognize their efforts. Make it a point, when there's a special program, for example, to honor them as guests. Let others know of their valuable service. Look at development as a people business, not as a business of simply raising dollars.

Capital Funds

There are other types of funding programs, of course, but almost all of them are based on and built from the annual giving program. There is a very definite need, on occasion, for the expansion or repair of buildings. In many instances that requires a capital campaign. An opportunity should be built into the capital campaign to expand the development program. The capital campaign should not simply achieve dollars for the building or for renovation, but the identification of new friends. These new allies can find out why the donors have committed financial resources and respond to those donors. All of this leads to the ability to generate funding on a deferred basis. Deferred dollars are given not simply as annual or capital gifts, but through bequests, wills, trusts and the like.

A high school board received a sizable gift through a charitable remainder trust. This was the first remainder trust gift ever made to this particular school. A man who had lived in the city all of his life, and who had no prior contact with the school made the gift. He had never been in the school before. He had no children attend the school. He had, however, on occasion been asked for annual gifts as part of the ongoing development program. Most importantly, one member of the board knew this gentleman and talked to him about why the school was important to that particular community and why he as a board member was devoting his time to it. The board member explained why, despite the fact that there were no longer Brothers available to staff the school, the school had a future and the school needed to exist to serve the community.

On the occasion of the opening of the new wing that was made possible by the gift, there was a reception which honored the man who made the gift. After the principal introduced him, the donor said, "I'm not here to be thanked; in fact the money is less important than your building a new science wing. I've been a medical doctor all of my life. People regularly ask me for money for all kinds of causes, but this is the first time that anyone has come to me and said that they wanted to talk about the importance of science in a Catholic school for boys. I've spent all of my life involved in science. I'm 73 now and retired. I want to thank you for giving me the opportunity to become involved in this school. I would consider it a great honor if in addition to accepting my gift, you will allow me to come in and talk to some of your classes in biology, in physics and in chemistry, about the importance of sciences." The school had raised a friend, not simply new funds. The doctor does in fact get invited back to school. He has become a part of it. That is what development is all about.

Summary   Development programs are designed to enhance the school through the attraction of people. They attract human resources as well as financial resources, with integrity and with commitment. Development allows you to attract resources not single-handedly, but through the involvement of people. Successful development programs cannot be run without the prerequisites discussed above. There needs to be at the very beginning an understanding, a commitment, an involvement, and a planning process that leads to a public statement of where you're going, and then an invitation to become involved in the exciting work of Catholic education.

Appendices

Understanding & Implementing
Development Programs in Catholic Schools

Good Development Requires Six Sequential Steps:
- UNDERSTANDING
- COMMITMENT
- INVOLVEMENT — BOARDS
- LONG-RANGE PLANNING
- A CASE STATEMENT
- FUNDING
  ANNUAL GIVING
  CAPITAL CAMPAIGNS
  TRUSTS & ENDOWMENTS
  DEFERRED GIVING

Introduction
With the increased interest in and emphasis on development programs in Catholic elementary and secondary schools, many administrators face decisions about when and how to establish such programs. Frequently there is early pressure to hire a Development Director, or immediately to plunge into fund raising events in order to give the impression of movement to the area of development.

Neither action will insure the success of the school's development program. Such hasty steps also may reflect a basic error of equating development with fund raising.

As used in our school system, the concept of development is much broader. It involves the clarification of the school's philosophy and goals, the ongoing effort to provide Catholic education of the highest quality, the communication of the school's values and achievements to its various publics, sound business management, and the effort to involve others

15

in support of the school's goals by their time, talent and financial assistance.

The intent of this summary is to clarify this understanding of development, and to provide the Catholic school administrator with a logical sequence of events which should be followed in establishing development programs. It is also the intent of this summary to provide information about reference materials which will explore individual subject areas in more depth. And finally, it is the intent of this summary to dispel the notion that a good development program requires the immediate hiring of paid staff in order to be successful.

Successful development does require that key leaders have a basic understanding of the development concept, as well as of the philosophy of Catholic education. However, successful development requires more than *understanding*. It also requires *commitment* on the part of key leaders, both to the philosophy of Catholic education and to the development concept. Moreover, successful development programs require the *involvement* of people, usually through the mechanism of representative boards.

It is only with that understanding, commitment and involvement that effective long range planning can be undertaken in an effort to insure that there is evidence that both quality Catholic education and good business management are taking place. With that evidence secured, the school Case statement can be developed and used to attract increasing numbers of people and dollars in support of the school's goals and objectives.

This summary briefly outlines those basic components and logical sequence of events necessary to the success of the development program, including: understanding, commitment, involvement, long range planning, Case statement and fund raising. Schools which have not followed steps in this sequence should go back and complete all steps as outlined in the process. Overlooked steps usually result in failure of the development process. It is our hope to explore these areas in greater detail in workshops and inservice programs in the future.

Understanding of

The Development Concept

Development defined—"The overall concept of development holds that the highest destiny of an institution can be realized only by a total effort on the part of the institution to analyze its philosophy, to crystallize its objectives, to project them into the future, and to take the necessary steps to realize them." (GGTS)[1,2]

The Philosphy of Catholic Education

"The integration of religious truth and values with the rest of life is brought about in the Catholic school not only by its unique curriculum but, more important, by the presence of teachers who express an integrated approach to learning and living in their private and professional lives. It is further reinforced by free interaction among the students themselves within their own community of youth." *(To Teach as Jesus Did ¶ 104)*[3]

The Development Process[4]

Formula for Implementation in Catholic Schools
- Evidence of Quality Catholic Education coupled with
- Evidence of Good Business Management coupled with
- Effective Marketing
- Attracts People and Dollars

BY:
Bishop
Diocesan Superintendent/Diocesan School Board
Pastor/Priest Director
Principal
Parish School Board Members

Commitment To: Philosophy of Catholic Education
Catholic Schools
Concept of Development

BY:
Bishop
Diocesan Superintendent/Diocesan School Board
Pastor/Priest Director
Principal
Parish School Board Members

Involvement Through The establishment, preservicing, inservicing and operation of the School Board.[5]
Catholic School Boards are a reflection of shared responsibility as it is understood in Church management. School

Boards act not only as a mechanism for involving people in the policy determinative process, but also provide an additional vehicle for parents to exercise their right and responsibility as primary educators of their children.

It is recommended that School Boards be established according to Diocesan guidelines.

It is extremely important that Board members have an opportunity to receive preservice in the areas of ministry, Catholic school philosophy, development and Board work. [6]

With the School Board established and the preservice program conducted, it is also important to establish an ongoing program of inservice (i.e., continuing education of the Board). It is generally recommended that one hour of inservice be scheduled at each Board meeting throughout the year. Generally, inservice programs should be given by members of the faculty and administration and touch on areas of philosophy, program, curriculum and extra-curricular activities.

Finally, it is recommended that the School Board work through a committee structure which would normally involve a limited number of standing committees such as those on long range planning, finance, plant and facilities, and development affairs.

BY:
Pastor/Priest Director
Principal
Faculty
Staff
Parents
Parishioners [7]

Long-Range Planning

Formal Five-Year Plan[8,9] covering the areas of:
- Philosophy
- Enrollment
- Curriculum
- Staffing
- Plant & Facilities
- Finances
- Development

Each section will include a supporting narrative covering the following perspectives:[10]

- Historical
- Current
- Future

The completed formal Five-Year Plan will include both narrative and backup materials designed to guide the administration and policy determinative Board in their work. The Plan is also designed to be updated annually, refining assumptions and continually looking five years ahead.

Long-Range Planning is prerequisite to both the creation of a Case Statement and to the ability of Catholic schools to flourish into the next century with an ability to attract both people and dollars.

Annual budgets and financial reports should be based on the Five-Year Plan and made available to the school's many "publics" as part of good business management in the Catholic school.

A Case Statement

A Case Statement is, most generally, a document designed for public distribution.[11] It is usually:

- Based on, reflective of, and a statement of the school's philosophy
- Based on the school's Five-Year Plan
- Prepared as a draft statement and received and reviewed by pastor, principal, Board, faculty and other involved publics
- Eventually prepared as a printed brochure
- Targeted to important publics such as alumni, grandparents, etc.

Funding

Types of funding programs include:[12]

- Annual Giving
- Deferred Giving
- Capital Giving
- Endowments

REFERENCES

[1] CSML II, 2

[2] "Development, The Flowering of Catholic Boardsmanship" *Policymaker,* Vol. 9, No. 4, June 1981 NCEA/NABE

[3] *To Teach as Jesus Did* Paragraph 104; The Catholic School* and Teach Them*

[4] CSML II, 2

[5] "Lay Leadership in Catholic Schools Dimensions and Dilemma" Robert R. Newton, *New Catholic World* March-April 1981

[6] CSML I, 4

[7] NCEA/NABE Cassette Tapes "An Inservice Program for Catholic Education Board may be ordered from NCEA/NABE, Suite 100, 1077 30th Street, N.W., Washington, DC 20007

[8] "Can Formal Long-Range Planning Solve Your School's Problems?" Richard J. Burke *Momentum,* October 1977

[9] "A Pragmatic Approach to the Teaching Ministry" Rev. Michael O'Neill *Momentum,* October 1977

[10] Appendix "B" Diocesan Guidelines for Long Range Planning

[11] CSML III, 3

[12] NCEA Development Booklets and CSML III, 4

Long Range Planning Guidelines for Catholic Schools

Long range planning is not simply a necessary component of good development. It is critically important to the ability of Catholic schools to survive and flourish through the 1980's, 1990's and beyond. It is an exercise of prudence, leadership and vision which articulates the goals of Catholic education for the school and organizes all available resources in a plan to attain those goals. Long range planning is an act of true Christian stewardship by which we strive to preserve and pass on to future generations the treasure of vital Catholic educational institutions.

Budgets have been described as a financial expression of the institution's priorities. So too, long range plans are meant to express the priorities and projections of the school in the areas of staffing, curriculum, enrollment, plant and facilities, as well as finance and development.

It is essential that all considerations in each of the above planning areas be based on and tied to the school's philosophy, reviewed in the light of the key related documents, namely, *To Teach As Jesus Did* (1972 Pastoral Message of the American Bishops), *The Catholic School* (1977 Statement of the Vatican Congregation for Catholic Education) and archdiocesan policies and guidelines.

The Principal's Role

It is the role of the principal, as the school administrator, to initiate the planning process and to guide it to completion. The pastor and priest director (if it is a parish school), and the school board should also be involved in the planning process. The "Suggested Chronology" on page 23 outlines the main steps of the planning process and the activities of those involved. (Further information on roles and responsibilities of those participating in the planning may be found in the *Catholic School Management Letter,* Vol. I, No. 4, February, 1980.)

Plan Format

The long range plan (five year plan) is designed not only to provide a direction for the school, but also a historical perspective for that direction. As a result, the narrative section of the long range plan should be completed in such a way that each major topic area discusses the historical perspective, the current situation, and assumptions which have been adopted for the future. In short, the narrative should attempt to answer these questions:

- Where have be been?
- Where are we today and why?
- Where are we going and why?
- How are we going to get there?

All of these should be related to the philosophy of Catholic education generally and the individual school particularly.

The narrative should support the projections made in each section of the plan (enrollment, curriculum, staffing, plant and facilities, and finance and development).

Again, it should be emphasized that care should be taken during each phase of the plan's creation to involve various individuals who have particular interest in and responsibility for that section of the plan.

Using the Long Range Plan

With the five year plan completed, it becomes a basic guideline document for the principal, pastor and Board. The plan should be reviewed, refined and updated on an *annual* basis so that it continually looks four years into the future.

It should be pointed out that the full five year plan is not designed for "public consumption." For that purpose a "case statement" based on the five year plan should be prepared which summarizes the assumptions made in each of the areas including enrollment, curriculum, staffing, plant and facilities, finance and development. The philosophy and mission statement of the school should also be clearly stated.

It is, of course, understood that every effort should be made during the planning process to insure that the curriculum and all aspects of the plan are reflective of the philosophy and that the values of Catholic education are well integrated with the curriculum.

Finally, the case statement should present investment opportunities which are well researched and supportable. These investment opportunities are designed to broaden the base of support for the school and to attract both people and dollars, i.e. to enlist the involvement of people with the school and to encourage their financial support.

Five year planning should be seen, not as an end in itself, but as a prerequisite to, and part of, good development, and as an important help to the school in attaining its goals.

Suggested Chronology For Developing A Five Year Plan

JULY
Principal/
Board Chairman

Set aside time for dreaming and goal setting. What problems and opportunities exist for the school? What should it be doing better? What ought it to emphasize now to be more faithful to its philosophy?

AUGUST
Pastor/Principal

Issue recommitment invitations to Board members. Make committee assignments. NOTE: During initial year provide Board members with *To Teach As Jesus Did, The Catholic School, Teach Them,* and the school's philosophy.
Arrange and conduct Board Preservice Program—include discussion of:
- Philosophy
- Roles & Responsibilities
- Distinction between policy making and administration.

Principal/ Board Chairman
- Pastor and Principal issue letter to Board commissioning Long Range Plan.

SEPTEMBER
Principal/Board Chairman

Convene Board or Long Range Plan Development Committee. Review basic assumptions constraints and timetable. Administrator shares dreams, problems and possibilities for school with Board. Board reviews school position in light of documents listed above, diocesan goals and school philosophy.

OCTOBER
Principal with School Board

Board reviews enrollment history and enrollment mix and begins creation of narrative citing reasons for enrollent changes.

Enrollment and/or Data Committee
- Collect and study prior five year enrollments by grade (department) and by religious category. (Catholic parishioners, Catholic non-parishioners, non-Catholics)
- Collect and study baptismal records for parishes for last five years.
- Compare baptismal records to "Parishioner enrollment" for appropriate years.
- Secure pertinent data from local public school officials concerning population trends in public school enrollment projections.
- Secure population trend information from Census Bureau, Chamber of Commerce, and telephone company.

- Build a five year enrollment projection based on all of the above (plan should be first by grade and then by religious mix). Be sure to consider current demographics, trends, health and fire codes as well as class size.
- Outline plans for market research as necessary and required.

NOVEMBER
Principal with Board

Board prepares enrollment projections for five years by grade level with accompanying narrative. A marketing plan for school "image" and enrollment should accompany enrollment projections in order to insure ability to achieve projections. (See *Catholic School Management Letter,* Volume 1, No. 3 & *Momentum,* May 1979, pgs. 42-45.)

DECEMBER
Principal/ Faculty

Curriculum section of five year plan to be completed by principal and faculty and presented for review by Board.
- Review and revise as needed, the school philosophy in light of *To Teach As Jesus Did* and *The Catholic School* and other documents cited and diocesan guidelines.
- Review current curriculum in light of diocesan guidelines and build a five year plan for curriculum updating as necessary.
- Include assumptions concerning textbooks (purchasing and replacement), library books, workbooks, equipment, teaching aids, audiovisual equipment, laboratory supplies, etc.
- Build a catalog of investment opportunities based on the dreams of the principal and staff. (See *Catholic School Management Letter,* Volume IV, 3)
- Evaluate program offerings including specialized areas (P.E., Music, Art, etc.)

JANUARY
Principal

Principal reviews current personnel records for all teachers (lay and Religious) and prepares for Board review a historical perspective and overview of current staffing situations, including qualifications, experience, salary, benefits, etc. Principal reviews staffing assumptions for next five years and prepares a summary for Board.

Principal/ Pastor/Board

Based on enrollment and staffing assumptions, the principal and Board prepare a five year projection for staffing by grade and/or department. Assumptions should be made in the areas of salaries and fringe benefits.

FEBRUARY
Principal/
Pastor/
Board Facilities
Committee

Initial plan for plant and facilities should be completed by a subcommittee of the Board working with the principal.

- Make a complete survey of all physical facilities available, including school buildings, residences and grounds. Based on current fire and health codes, list all necessary and desirable repairs and capital improvements.
- Develop a five year plan to complete improvements. Include cost estimates. Survey should be specific as to the number of classrooms and specialized areas to be utilized.
- Build a catalog of investment opportunities based on capital improvements and repairs to buildings, grounds, furniture and equipment.

MARCH
Principal/
Pastor/
Board Finance
Committee

Review school costs for the last three years (using annual reports).

- Insure that all line items are exclusively school and not attributable to other parish or religious education programs.
- Develop an expenditure budget based on enrollment, curriculum, staffing, plant and facility considerations. (Financial growth assumptions should be clearly stated in footnotes or in assumptions section of plan.) Include provision for some level of student assistance.

APRIL
Principal/
Pastor/
Board Finance
Committee

Develop a five-year income plan with realistic assumptions in the areas of tuition, subsidies, traditional fund raising, and investment opportunities. Create a five-year development plan.

MAY
Board

Review the completed five-year plan including projections and accompanying narrative in areas of philosophy, enrollment, curriculum, staffing, plant and facilities, and finances and development.

- Approval of final five-year plan by Board.

JUNE
Principal/
Board

Preparation of summary "Case Statement" and Development Plan, based on five-year plan, to be used in promoting the school to various publics. (Note: may take more than one month.)

- Identify Case Statement—summary of history, philosophy, vision and objectives in a manner that invites credibility and investment. This statement should stress unique and desirable characteristics of the total educational program,

especially through elements related to its identity as a Catholic school.
- Identify for past five years:
  —Alumni relations
  —Public relations
  —Special gifts
  —Publics being served
  —Endowments
  —Foundation grants
  —Business/Industry participation
  —Estate Planning (bequests)
  —Insurance gifts
  —Fund raising projects
- Identify priorities for the next five years.
- Project realistic involvement and dollar increase to support Finance Committee projections.
- Establish appropriate committees to respond to five-year priority selections.

NOTE: It is assumed that in fulfillment of the planning role assigned to him/her above, the principal will involve the faculty, through frequent consultation and other appropriate ways.

The following forms are available in 8-1/2" × 11" format as an Appendix to a larger book entitled Elementary School Finance Manual. Those interested may obtain this book from the Publications Sales Office, NCEA. The cost is $10.00.

Enrollment History

(School Name, Town) _____

Grade	1980-81	1981-82	1982-83	1983-84
Pre K				
K				
1				
2				
3				
4				
5				
6				
7				
8				
TOTALS				

Enrollment by Grade

(School Name, Town) _____

	Grade	Projections			
Grade	1984-85	1985-86	1986-87	1987-88	1988-89
Pre K					
K					
1					
2					
3					
4					
5					
6					
7					
8					
TOTALS					

Enrollment Mix

(School Name, Town) _____

				Number of Children			
Category	# of Children Per Family	1984-85 # of Families	1984-85 # of Children	1985-86	1986-87	1987-88	1988-89
Parishioners	1	× _____	= _____	_____	_____	_____	_____
	2	× _____	= _____	_____	_____	_____	_____
	3	× _____	= _____	_____	_____	_____	_____
	4	× _____	= _____	_____	_____	_____	_____
	5 or more	× _____	= _____	_____	_____	_____	_____
		SUB-TOTAL	_____	_____	_____	_____	_____
Catholic Non-Parishioners	1	× _____	= _____	_____	_____	_____	_____
	2	× _____	= _____	_____	_____	_____	_____
	3	× _____	= _____	_____	_____	_____	_____
	4	× _____	= _____	_____	_____	_____	_____
	5 or more	× _____	= _____	_____	_____	_____	_____
		SUB-TOTAL	_____	_____	_____	_____	_____
Non-Catholics	1	× _____	= _____	_____	_____	_____	_____
	2	× _____	= _____	_____	_____	_____	_____
	3	× _____	= _____	_____	_____	_____	_____
	4	× _____	= _____	_____	_____	_____	_____
	5 or more	× _____	= _____	_____	_____	_____	_____
		SUB-TOTAL	_____	_____	_____	_____	_____
		TOTAL ENROLLMENT	_____	_____	_____	_____	_____

Staffing Detail

(School Name, Town) _____

Name	Grade/Subject Taught	Professional Preparation and Interests	Certification YES NO	Current Salary	Year Started Teaching	Year Started In School

Staff Benefit Detail

(Check appropriate columns)

(School Name, Town) _____

Name	Grade/Subject Taught	B/C Single Family	Medical B/S Single Family	Major Medical Single Family	Life Ins.	Retire.	TSA	Other Coverage Provided by School

Staffing by Grade

(Number of Teachers per grade and Salary)

(School Name, Town) _____

Grade	Actual 1984-85 Religious (#) ($)	Lay (#) ($)	Projections 1985-86 Religious (#) ($)	Lay (#) ($)	1986-87 Religious (#) ($)	Lay (#) ($)	1987-88 Religious (#) ($)	Lay (#) ($)	1988-89 Religious (#) ($)	Lay (#) ($)
Pre K										
K										
1										
2										
3										
4										
5										
6										
7										
8										
Principal										
Others										
TOTALS										

Tuition Detail

(School Name, Town) _____

		Actual	Projections			
		1984-85 Tuition	1985-86 Tuition	1986-87 Tuition	1987-88 Tuition	1988-89 Tuition
Parishioners	1					
	2					
	3					
	4					
	5 or more					
Catholic Non-Parishioners	1					
	2					
	3					
	4					
	5 or more					
Non-Catholics	1					
	2					
	3					
	4					
	5 or more					

Five Year Development Plan

Place in the boxes the task or objective to be accomplished that year in an effort to improve the overall development position of the school.

	1984-85	1985-86	1986-87	1987-88	1988-89
QUALITY CATHOLIC EDUCATION					
BUSINESS MANAGEMENT					
PUBLIC RELATIONS					
PARENT-STUDENT FUNDRAISING					
ALUMNI ACTIVITIES AND FUNDRAISING					

Note: Cite Specific Activities

Five Year Development Plan

Place in the boxes the task or objective to be accomplished that year in an effort to improve the overall development position of the school.

	1984-85	1985-86	1986-87	1987-88	1988-89
ANNUAL GIVING PROGRAMS (OTHER THAN PARENTS AND ALUMNI)					
BUSINESS AND COMMUNITY CULTIVATION & INVESTMENT					
NEWSLETTERS AND OTHER COMMUNICATIONS VEHICLES					
FOUNDATION GRANTS					
ENDOWMENT PROGRAM (ESTABLISHMENT OF ADVISORY COMMITTEE AND PROGRAM)					

Note: Cite Specific Activities

31

Parish Elementary School — Five Year Plan

(School Name, Town) _____

SCHOOL INCOME	Budget 1984-85	Projections 1985-86	1986-87	1987-88	1988-89
TUITION					
a. Kindergarten	_____	_____	_____	_____	_____
b. Parishioners	_____	_____	_____	_____	_____
c. Non-Parishioners, Catholic family	_____	_____	_____	_____	_____
d. Non-Catholics	_____	_____	_____	_____	_____
e. (Contingency for uncollectable tuition)	(_____)	(_____)	(_____)	(_____)	(_____)
TOTAL of: a, b, c, d, (minus e)	_____	_____	_____	_____	_____
ASSESSMENT FROM PARISHES OF NON-PARISHIONERS	_____	_____	_____	_____	_____
FEES (Graduation, Registration, etc.)	_____	_____	_____	_____	_____
GIFTS, ENDOWMENTS	_____	_____	_____	_____	_____
SUBSIDY FROM PARISH	_____	_____	_____	_____	_____
ALL OTHER INCOME					
a. Cafeteria — Milk Program (Include student payment & federal subsidy)	_____	_____	_____	_____	_____
b. Collection drives for school	_____	_____	_____	_____	_____
c. Parent & Student fund raising activities	_____	_____	_____	_____	_____
d. Other sources	_____	_____	_____	_____	_____
TOTAL of: a, b, c, d.	_____	_____	_____	_____	_____
DEVELOPMENT INCOME	_____	_____	_____	_____	_____
TOTAL SCHOOL INCOME	$ _____	$ _____	$ _____	$ _____	$ _____

School Expenses

	Actual	Projections			
	1984-85	1985-86	1986-87	1987-88	1988-89
INSTRUCTIONAL SALARIES (Exclude employer's share of Social Security)					
a. Lay teachers & lay principals					
b. Religious teachers & principals					
c. Substitutes					
d. Social Security (Employer Share)					
e. Lay Emp. Benefit Program (Employer Share)					
f. Unemployment Compensation					
TOTAL of: a, b, c, d, e, f					
INSTRUCTION—OTHER					
a. Textbooks & Workbooks — secular					
b. Textbooks & Workbooks — religious					
c. Library books & supplies					
d. Teaching supplies & AV supplies					
e. Office supplies & expense					
TOTAL of: a, b, c, d, e					
OPERATIONS, SALARIES					
a. Custodian					
b. Office Staff					
TOTAL of: a, b					
OPERATIONS, OTHER					
a. Fuel					
b. Electricity, water, gas, phone					
c. Custodial supplies					
d. Custodial services (Contracted)					
TOTAL of: a, b, c, d					
MAINTENANCE					
a. Building repairs					
b. Scheduled maintenance					
c. Repair & replacement of furn., equip.					
TOTAL of: a, b, c					
FIXED CHARGES					
a. Property Insurance					
b. Pupil insurance					
c. Teacher Inservice					
d. Other fixed costs					
TOTAL of: a, b, c, d					
STUDENT SERVICES					
a. Cafeteria — Milk Program					
b. Extra-curricular activities					
c. Other — miscellaneous					
TOTAL of: a, b, c					
TOTAL SCHOOL EXPENSES	$	$	$	$	$
TOTAL CONVENT EXPENSES (cf. p. 97)	$	$	$	$	$
TOTAL EXPENSES (School & Convent)	$	$	$	$	$

SAMPLE

Convent Expenses

	Actual	Projections			
	1984-85	1985-86	1986-87	1987-88	1988-89
CONVENT EXPENSES					
Domestic (salary)					
Auto expense (If paid by parish/school)					
Fuel, electricity, water, gas, phone ..					
Repairs					
Property Insurance					
Health Insurance — Sisters (If paid by parish/school)					
Rental, non-parish residence for Sisters					
Equip., furn., improvements					
Other convent expenses					
TOTAL CONVENT EXPENSES	$	$	$	$	$
SCHOOL STATISTICS					
Total School Enrollment					
Total number of classrooms in the building					
Total number of classrooms used for school purposes					

Grades offered and grade enrollment (Insert grade enrollment on line and number of classrooms per grade in parentheses)

					1984-85 Total Enrollment
1984-85					
K _____ ( ), 1 _____ ( ), 2 _____ ( ), 3 _____ ( ), 4 _____ ( ),					
5 _____ ( ), 6 _____ ( ), 7 _____ ( ), 8 _____ ( ), 9 _____ ( )					

					1985-86 Total Enrollment
1985-86					
K _____ ( ), 1 _____ ( ), 2 _____ ( ), 3 _____ ( ), 4 _____ ( ),					
5 _____ ( ), 6 _____ ( ), 7 _____ ( ), 8 _____ ( ), 9 _____ ( )					

					1986-87 Total Enrollment
1986-87					
K _____ ( ), 1 _____ ( ), 2 _____ ( ), 3 _____ ( ), 4 _____ ( ),					
5 _____ ( ), 6 _____ ( ), 7 _____ ( ), 8 _____ ( ), 9 _____ ( )					

					1987-88 Total Enrollment
1987-88					
K _____ ( ), 1 _____ ( ). 2 _____ ( ), 3 _____ ( ), 4 _____ ( ),					
5 _____ ( ), 6 _____ ( ), 7 _____ ( ), 8 _____ ( ), 9 _____ ( )					

					1988-89 Total Enrollment
1988-89					
K _____ ( ), 1 _____ ( ), 2 _____ ( ), 3 _____ ( ), 4 _____ ( ),					
5 _____ ( ), 6 _____ ( ), 7 _____ ( ), 8 _____ ( ), 9 _____ ( )					